Connect

The Key To "Meant All Health" Recovery

It's A Rap

A lifestyle Choice

By Olivia Johnson

Copyright © 2021 Olivia Johnson

First Edition 2021

ISBN: 9798500145673

Disconnect

Mental Health

Reconnect

Mental Health

A

Theme

Underpinning the dream

Of Good Mental Health

Conscious Connect

Subconscious Disconnect

Hard to see

A Lifestyle Choice

A Recovery Voice

Conscious out of Sync?

Subconscious out of Sync?

Two cogs at odds

Poor Mental Health

That's How It Felt

Therapy?

Counselling?

Or Self Development?

See the Coggs

How they work

Together

Or Not?

Where is the Rot

Cognitive Dissonance?

At a glance

Is there a chance?

What about

Lance?

Go in and see

Express yourself

Connect

Let yourself be known

Conscious

Subconscious

Be brave

Be courageous

It is only you

Delve deep

That is neat

Allow

Be Kind

Let your mind

Let you

Explore

Be Kind

In the mind

Read Insight

Delight

Let the journey begin

You are not afraid

It is all ok

Connect within

To see the sin

To see the din

That might not

Belong to you

Whilst connecting

Within

Connect outside

Keep alive

Connect

Anything to Connect

A friend

Family

Collecting online

Painting fine

Running or jogging

Exercise?

Diet?

Meditation?

Nature?

You name it

You do it

Let it be right

Connect

Emotional

Support

Caring

Daring

Who is it

Going to be?

Vital

For Recovery

Recover

Insight

Delight

Not Trite

Phone a friend

A friend phones you

Out of the blue?

Go for a walk

Go for a talk

Go for a swim

Go for a win

Talk it through

With someone

You know

Don't let yourself go

Let yourself grow

Connect

Webcam live

Venice

A beach

A treat

Connect

Spur yourself on

Diarise Events

Look forward to TV

Bid online

Watch sport

Read a book

Go for a power walk

Go for a cycle

Run for fun

Five a side football

Online learning

Connect

Connect

Connect

It's best

While you rest

While you gain Insight

While you recover

Keep afloat

Don't rock the boat

Keep the medication

Keep the dedication

Handle it well

Avoid a frightening spell

Manage it

Let others help you to

Manage it

Your not alone

Don't be alone

Find Help

Open up

Be bold

Trust

Others will help

Others can help

Some Understand

Qualified Professionals

Are there

They really care

Let them hold your hand

Let them be a support

As you gain insight

As you cope

Don't rock the boat

Be full of hope

You will gain insight

You will get to know

The way out will appear

Gradually each step

One at a time

It may cost a dime

That's just right at the time

So that you can be sublime

While progressing in rhyme

Recover yourself

Focus on that

And see how it works

It is a process

That will lead to improvements

Untold

That will eventually

Make you free

Just to be you

Without the past

Baggage

So you can travel

Full of light

And be full of right

In the question

At night

And Don't be a sprite!

About The Author

The Author realised over many decades of experiencing Mental Health issues that her main reason for

this happening was because of some sort of Disconnection within herself, within her mind. She was leading

An Empty Life.

A disconnection or difference between her subconscious and her conscious

- **Aligning back her subconscious with her conscious through Insight or Awareness**

  Was the key to her Mental Health Journey of Recovery

The author experienced **emotional neglect in childhood** from a very young age.

She happened to find herself on a continual mental health recovery journey in her early 30's,

Through no fault of her own.

She was **experiencing an empty life**. And then she discovered what was needed was a Lifestyle choice.

The choice to dedicate herself to her own Mental Health Recovery with the help of her friends and family.

Disclaimer

This book is designed to provide information and motivation to its readers.

It is sold with the understanding that neither the publisher nor author are engaged to provide any type of

psychological, legal or any other kind of professional mental health advice.

It is purely an expression of the author's own personal mental health journey and her or his reflections

upon it, and not that of the publisher.

Neither the publisher nor the author shall be liable for any physical, psychological, emotional,

financial or commercial damages including, but not limited to special, incidental, consequential or other damages.

Our views and rights are the same.

The reader is responsible for their own choices, actions and results as a result of reading this book.

Printed in Great Britain
by Amazon